Red Indians

History, Life, and Culture of Native American Tribes

Dr. Paul O. Titus

Library of Congress Cataloging-in-Publication Data
Titus, Paul O.
The Red Indians: History, Life, and Culture of Native American Tribes / Dr. Paul O. Titus.

First Edition, 2025

Printed in the United States of America

Acknowledgment

Writing The Red Indians – History, Life, and Culture of Native American Tribes has been both an enlightening and humbling journey. This book would not have been possible without the guidance, encouragement, and support of many individuals and communities.

First and foremost, I express my deepest gratitude to the Native American tribes whose resilience, traditions, and wisdom inspired this work. Their stories and cultural legacies are the heartbeat of this book.

I am thankful to the historians, anthropologists, and cultural scholars whose research and writings provided valuable insights and helped me frame this narrative with both respect and accuracy.

To my family and friends, your patience, encouragement, and belief in me kept this project alive through countless hours of research and writing.

Finally, I dedicate this work to future generations, with the hope that it fosters understanding, respect, and appreciation for the enduring spirit of the Native American people.

— Dr. Paul O. Titus

Table of contents

The First Footprints: Where It All Began 8

Life Woven with the Land 9

Spirituality: Walking with the Great Spirit 10

Traditions and Storytelling 11

Daily Life: A World of Work and Celebration 11

Survival in the Face of Struggle 12

Modern Struggles and Enduring Spirit 13

Chapter Two Life, Spirit, and Daily Practice: How Communities Lived Before
Contact 15

A Day in the Village 15

Homes and Material Life 16

Foodways and Agriculture 17

Gender, Leadership, and Social Roles 18

Health, Healing, and Medicine 19

Education and Transmission of Knowledge 20

Spiritual Life and Ritual 21

Art, Symbol, and Meaning 21

Festivals, Law, and Social Justice 22

Practical Lessons for Today 22

Passing the Torch 23

Chapter Three Contact with Europeans: First Meetings, Disease, and Survival 25

The First Meetings 25

Trade and Technology: New Goods, New Dependencies 26

The Invisible Enemy: Disease and Demographic Collapse 27

Diplomacy, Alliances, and the Price of Peace *28*

Culture in Motion: Adaptation and Resistance *29*

Missionaries, Schools, and the Attack on Culture *30*

Land, Law, and the Erosion of Territory *30*

Survival Strategies that Endured *31*

Stories of Response *32*

Practical Lessons for Readers *33*

Looking Ahead *33*

Chapter Four The Struggle for Survival: Wars, Removals, and Resilience *35*

When Peace Turned to Conflict *35*

Forced Removals and Broken Promises *36*

War and Massacre *36*

Law as a Tool of Dispossession *37*

The Attack on Culture: Schools and Assimilation *38*

Economic Displacement and Everyday Survival *39*

Cultural Preservation and Adaptation *40*

Leadership and Resistance Movements *40*

Small Acts That Kept Culture Alive *41*

Stories of Resilience *41*

Practical Steps for Readers *42*

Looking Ahead *43*

Chapter Five Legacy, Resilience, and Modern Identity *44*

Carrying the Past into the Present *44*

Legal and Political Turnarounds *45*

Cultural Revival and Language Reclamation *46*

Arts, Literature, and New Voices 47

Economic Self-Determination 48

Environmental Leadership and Stewardship 48

Youth, Identity, and the Future 49

Ongoing Challenges 50

Practical Ways Readers Can Support Renewal 50

Stories That Point the Way 51

Looking Ahead 52

Chapter Six Language, Land, and Law: Reclaiming What Was Lost 54

The Sound of Return: Language Revival 54

Land Back: Buybacks, Monuments, and Return 56

Courts and Treaties: Law as a Tool for Redress 57

How These Threads Strengthen Each Other 58

Concrete Examples and Resources 59

Practical Steps for Readers Who Want to Help 60

Stories That Point the Way 61

Looking Ahead 61

*Chapter Seven — New Voices: Art, Literature, and the Public Return of Indigenous
Story* 64

When Tradition Meets Gallery Space 64

Storytellers: Novelists, Poets, and the Native Renaissance 65

Performance and the Powwow Stage 66

Film, Music, and Media: Reclaiming the Camera and Microphone 67

Where Art Meets Activism 68

Young Creators and the Future of Tradition 69

Practical Steps for Readers Who Want to Engage 70

Stories That Teach 71

Visual Elements and Practical Resources 71

Looking Ahead 72

Chapter Eight Honor, Hope, and What Comes Next: Modern Identity and the Road Forward 73

Identity in Motion 73

The New Commons: Culture as Collective Strength 74

Young People as Cultural Stewards 74

Sovereignty, Governance, and Practical Power 75

Economic Choices That Respect Culture 76

Environmental Stewardship and Climate Resilience 77

Healing Work: Addressing Intergenerational Trauma 78

The Role of Allies: How Non-Indigenous Readers Can Help 78

Practical Steps Readers Can Do Right Now 79

Stories That Point to a Better Future 80

Toward a Living Conclusion 80

Printable Two-Page Handout 83

Carrying the Story Forward — Practical Resources and Actions 83

One-Page Reading Guide for Book Groups 88

The Red Indians — Quick Book Group Guide 88

Chapter One
The Origins and Early Journeys of the Red Indians

Long before the world came to know the Americas as "the New World," vast lands stretched across two continents, untouched by European sails or African slave ships. Rolling plains, towering mountains, dense forests, and winding rivers gave life to countless communities that called these lands home. These were the First Peoples—the Native Americans, often called the "Red Indians" in earlier times. Their story is not only about survival but also about spirit, resilience, and an unbreakable bond with the earth itself.

The First Footprints: Where It All Began

*The origins of Native American peoples are deeply fascinating. Scholars believe that tens of thousands of years ago, during the last Ice Age, massive sheets of ice locked up much of the Earth's water. This caused sea levels to drop, exposing a land bridge known as **Beringia** between Siberia and Alaska. Across this frozen highway, small bands of hunter-gatherers journeyed, following mammoths, bison, and caribou. They did not know they were walking into what would later become a vast, unexplored continent.*

For centuries, migration continued. Families pushed southward into fertile valleys, hunting grounds, and coastal areas. They adapted to every environment—from the icy Arctic tundra of the

Inuit, to the deserts of the Southwest, to the forests of the East. Over thousands of years, they developed unique languages, customs, and ways of life.

*What makes this migration remarkable is how it shaped a **shared identity of resilience**. Each step into new terrain meant learning fresh ways to survive. In the dry plains, they became buffalo hunters. In the forests, they became skilled farmers. Along the coasts, they turned to fishing and canoe-making. Survival was never just about food—it was about learning to live in harmony with nature's rhythm.*

Life Woven with the Land

For the Native peoples, land was never just property. It was sacred, a living force that nourished and guided them. To them, the earth was not something to own but something to honor. Rivers were lifelines, mountains were guardians, and animals were teachers.

Take the Plains tribes as an example. The buffalo was at the heart of their existence. It provided food, clothing, shelter, and tools. Yet, every hunt was done with deep respect. Before killing a buffalo, hunters would offer prayers, thanking the animal's spirit. Nothing was wasted—bones became weapons, hides became lodges, and sinew became thread. This balance of give-and-take reflected a worldview that saw all life as connected.

This spiritual bond extended beyond hunting. Farming tribes, such as the Hopi and Iroquois, planted corn, beans, and squash—known as the "Three Sisters." These crops grew best together, supporting each other in the soil just as families supported one another in the community. To Native peoples, farming was not just labor; it was a sacred act, a partnership with the earth.

Spirituality: Walking with the Great Spirit

*At the heart of Native life was spirituality. Most tribes believed in a **Great Spirit**, a creator who gave life to the world and guided human destiny. But this belief was not distant or abstract. The Great Spirit lived in the wind, the rivers, the animals, and even in dreams.*

*Ceremonies and rituals played a central role. The Lakota people, for example, performed the **Sun Dance**, a ritual of sacrifice, renewal, and connection with the divine. The Navajo created beautiful sand paintings during healing ceremonies, believing that these designs opened a path to spiritual balance.*

Shamans, or medicine men and women, were highly respected. They acted as healers, storytellers, and spiritual guides. Through chants, herbs, and visions, they sought harmony not just for individuals but for the entire tribe.

Spirituality wasn't separated from daily life—it was woven into it. Every hunt, every harvest, every birth and death was seen as part of a spiritual cycle. This deep sense of connection gave Native peoples the strength to endure hardship and meaning to their survival.

Traditions and Storytelling

If you were to sit by a fire in a Native village centuries ago, you would quickly understand the importance of stories. Elders told tales of creation, of heroes and tricksters, of victories and defeats. These stories were more than entertainment; they were lessons, histories, and moral compasses.

For example, the Cherokee told stories of the first fire, teaching not just about survival but also about the values of cooperation and respect. Trickster tales, like those of Coyote or Raven, often carried warnings about greed, arrogance, or disobedience.

These oral traditions bound communities together, ensuring that knowledge passed from one generation to the next. They also preserved identity. Even when tribes faced war, displacement, and hardship, their stories reminded them of who they were and where they came from.

Daily Life: A World of Work and Celebration

Life in Native villages was full of rhythm—hard work balanced with moments of celebration.

Men often hunted, fished, and defended the tribe, while women farmed, prepared food, and crafted clothing and tools. Yet these roles were not rigid; in many tribes, women held significant power. Among the Iroquois, for instance, women chose the chiefs and could even remove them if they failed to lead wisely.

Homes reflected the environment. The Plains tribes built **tipis**, *portable cone-shaped tents that could be moved with the buffalo herds. The Pueblo peoples built* **adobe houses**, *sturdy and cool against the desert heat. The Iroquois lived in longhouses, where entire families shared space under one roof.*

Celebrations were equally important. Feasts, dances, and ceremonies marked every stage of life—from harvest festivals to naming rituals for newborns. Music filled the air with drums, flutes, and chants, each sound carrying spiritual meaning.

Survival in the Face of Struggle

For centuries, Native peoples thrived across the Americas. But survival was never easy. Harsh winters, droughts, and scarcity of food often tested their strength. Yet they adapted with remarkable resilience.

When food was scarce, tribes shared resources. When enemies attacked, they formed alliances. When new challenges arose, they created new tools, weapons, and strategies. This ability to adapt became their greatest weapon for survival.

But the greatest challenge was yet to come. In the late 15th century, European ships would cross the Atlantic, bringing not only new goods but also disease, warfare, and displacement. The arrival of strangers would forever alter the story of Native America.

Modern Struggles and Enduring Spirit

Today, the story of Native peoples is not just one of the past. It is also about the present. Colonization, forced removals, and cultural erasure have left lasting scars. Many tribes lost their lands, languages, and traditions. Poverty, discrimination, and health challenges remain real struggles.

Yet, Native communities continue to fight for recognition and survival. Efforts to preserve languages, revive ceremonies, and reclaim ancestral lands are ongoing. Powwows celebrate culture with dance, song, and unity. Young generations are reconnecting with traditions, blending them with modern life.

This resilience is perhaps the greatest lesson of all. Despite centuries of hardship, Native peoples remain strong, proud, and deeply connected to their roots. Their story reminds us that survival is not just about living through hardship—it is about carrying forward identity, spirit, and hope.

Chapter Two
Life, Spirit, and Daily Practice: How Communities Lived Before Contact

If Chapter One was about where the first peoples came from, this chapter is about how they lived. It looks at the daily rhythms that shaped village life, the spiritual practices that guided decisions, and the cultural systems that gave meaning to work, family, and community. These were not isolated customs. Each habit, tool, and ceremony fit into a larger pattern that kept communities healthy, taught the young, and tied people to the land. To understand Native life is to see a world where the practical and the sacred were inseparable.

A Day in the Village

Picture a small settlement at dawn. Smoke rises from earthen ovens. A woman stokes the fire and checks a pot of stewed corn. Children wake and stretch. A father sharpens a spear for a morning hunt. An elder walks to the central gathering place to meet a council member. Work and ritual start together.

Daily tasks varied by environment and by the roles each person carried, but a few common threads run through many communities. People woke to work that mattered. Food preparation, toolmaking, farming, weaving, trading, and teaching filled the day. The labor was purposeful and shared. Those who could carry heavy loads did so. Those who cared well for children and elders performed work of equal value.

Work was often seasonal. Planting and harvesting demanded long hours in the field. Winter demanded mending, storytelling, and indoor crafts. Summer brought trading and long-distance travel. Life adjusted to the cycles of weather and growth. That adjustment was not a burden. It was a rhythm that connected people to the year.

Homes and Material Life

Homes reflected the environment and lifestyle. On the Plains, tipis were elegant solutions. They packed flat and rose quickly, matching a mobile way of life that followed buffalo herds. Tipis breathed. A central smoke hole let fires burn for warmth and cooking. Inside, hides, woven mats, and fur bedding kept families warm.

In the Southwest, pueblos rose from clay and stone. Their thick walls shaded interiors from the punishing sun and held cool air into the evening. Multiroom houses meant extended families could live together. Roofs became places for drying corn and for private conversation.

In the Eastern Woodlands, longhouses sheltered multiple family units under a single roof. These large structures supported communal living. Inside, smoke from a dozen hearths simmered with stews, and the hum of trade and storytelling connected kin by a practical intimacy.

Material culture extended beyond shelter. Clothes, baskets, pottery, and tools were made by hand and meant to last. Women and men had complementary skills. Basket weaving taught patience and pattern recognition. Pottery required an eye for heat and balance. Tools were shaped from bone, stone, wood, and eventually metal. Craftsmanship was a teaching method. When a child learned to sew or to fish, they were also learning history.

Foodways and Agriculture

Food shaped everything. In some regions, agriculture anchored life. The "Three Sisters" planting method of corn, beans, and squash is a famous example, but there were many local systems that served the same purpose. Corn provided a sturdy backbone. Beans restored nitrogen to the soil and climbed the corn stalks. Squash shaded soil and deterred weeds with broad leaves. Together, they represented a living partnership in the garden and a lesson in cooperation.

In fishing communities along coasts and rivers, nets and weirs displayed technological skill. Along the Northwest Coast, rich salmon runs supported dense populations and complex myth cycles. In the interior, root crops, nuts, and wild fruits supplemented meat from hunts.

Hunting itself involved deep practical knowledge. Tracking an animal meant reading the land. Hunters understood seasons, wind patterns, and animal behavior. Sustainable hunting practices were common. Many communities hunted only what they needed. Rituals before and after a hunt reinforced respect. The animal was thanked and honored, with as much of it used as possible.

Food storage was another skill entirely. Drying, smoking, and processing allowed communities to survive tough winters. Community granaries and shared stores smoothed out the lean years. These systems implied trust and social bonds. A family in need could be fed by neighbors. That social safety net mattered as much as the harvest itself.

Gender, Leadership, and Social Roles

Roles were practical and flexible. Gender divisions existed, but they did not always map onto rigid hierarchies. In many nations, women were leaders in their own right. They tended land, controlled seed distribution, and guided domestic and spiritual life. Among the Haudenosaunee, or Iroquois, clan mothers held power to nominate and remove chiefs. That balance shows a political order that valued consensus and accountability.

Men might lead hunting parties and war parties, but leadership was earned through service. Elders held authority because they carried knowledge. Children learned respect by watching. Social order grew out of community needs, not abstract law.

Trade networks also shaped social life. Long before Europeans arrived, extensive trade routes connected tribes. Shells from the Atlantic ended up in the heartland. Obsidian and copper moved over great distances. Trade made people neighbors with the faraway. It also spread ideas, songs, and technologies. Diplomatic skills mattered. A chief's role could include mediating disputes and arranging marriages that strengthened ties.

Health, Healing, and Medicine

Health practices were both practical and spiritual. Herbal knowledge was extensive. Roots, barks, and leaves treated wounds, fevers, and digestive troubles. Midwives brought babies into the world in settings shaped by ritual and care. Healers used a *mixture of herbal remedies, massage, and spiritual techniques.*

Medicine men and women, often called shamans, played central roles. Their training combined observation with apprenticeship. They read dreams, visited the spirit world, and performed ceremonies to restore balance. Illness was often understood as a disruption of harmony. Healing aimed at restoring that balance within the individual and in relation to community and cosmos.

This worldview produced medical strategies that were holistic. Treating a wound involved cleaning the injury and also addressing grief or social conflict that might have destabilized a person's spirit. This approach did not replace practical wound care. It supplemented it with a wider sense of health.

Education and Transmission of Knowledge

Children learned in context. Education happened through participation. A child accompanying a parent was absorbing skills by imitation. Storytelling taught ethics, history, and identity. Songs encoded genealogies. Practical tasks taught math and science in a hands-on way. A young potter learned geometry by watching a wheel. A hunter learned timing and weather by following migratory birds.

Initiation rituals marked maturity and transferred responsibility. These rites signaled readiness to take on adult roles. They often included instruction on cultural values, survival techniques, and spiritual responsibilities. The process was communal. Elders tested, taught, and blessed the next generation.

Spiritual Life and Ritual

Spirit was everywhere. Rituals mapped life. Births, naming, marriages, hunts, and deaths were all invested with ceremonial meaning. The goal was maintaining balance and honoring relationships.

Many ceremonies celebrated seasons. Planting and harvest seasons came with prayers of gratitude. Music and dance bound people together. Drums set a communal heartbeat. Flutes, rattles, and call-and-response singing created a shared emotional landscape.

Sacred landscapes mattered. Mountains, springs, groves, and rivers were places of pilgrimage. They held stories of creation and of ancestors. For many tribes, the land itself taught. A rock might mark a birth story. A river could tell of migration and loss. Spiritual practice intertwined history and place.

Art, Symbol, and Meaning

Art was practical and symbolic. Patterns on a basket pointed to clan identity. Totem poles told family stories. Beadwork recorded births and marriages. Tattoos could mark achievements. Artifacts were not museum objects. They were living signs.

Art preserved memory. Symbols carried teachings about relationships with animals, the weather, and other people. A painted animal could be a prayer for a successful hunt. A carved mask might call spirits to a healing ceremony. Artistic practice taught manual skills and encoded cosmology.

Festivals, Law, and Social Justice

Customs enforced order. Social norms had teeth. Shame and praise were powerful regulators. The law was often restorative rather than punitive. A person who violated a community agreement might be asked to compensate or to do service for those harmed. Public processes allowed debate and remediation. That approach prioritized community health.

Festivals reinforced solidarity. They were times for feasting, reconciliation, and alliance building. In such gatherings, old disputes could be resolved. New agreements were formed. The community celebrated its capacity to survive and to renew.

Practical Lessons for Today

There is pragmatic wisdom to borrow. Here are a few practical steps readers can consider.

1. *Learn by doing. Visit a tribal museum and attend a hands-on workshop in pottery, weaving, or traditional plant use. Practical engagement teaches faster and more respectfully than mere observation.*
2. *Support living artists and makers. Buy beadwork, textiles, and books from Native creators. Economic support sustains culture.*
3. *Learn a few words in a local Indigenous language. Even small efforts demonstrate respect and open doors to deeper learning.*
4. *Practice seasonal awareness. Try growing a small garden or plan meals around local, seasonal produce. It is a small way to test how ecosystems and human life relate.*
5. *Read contemporary Native authors. Voices from within a culture give a perspective that secondhand accounts cannot.*

These are small steps, but they change how you move through the world. They shift curiosity into a relationship.

Passing the Torch

This chapter has tried to bring daily life into focus. The buffer of time and distance can make ancient habits feel exotic, but many of the principles are strikingly practical. Purposeful work, community support, respect for the land, and balanced spiritual life made these societies durable.

What follows is not inevitable. The arrival of Europeans would test these systems in ways never imagined. The next chapter will trace first contact, the exchange of goods and ideas, and the shock of disease and displacement. It is a story of unexpected consequences and of the long struggle to maintain culture in the face of rapid and violent change.

As we move into that turbulent chapter, keep in mind the everyday world we have just examined. It is the foundation on which subsequent resistance, adaptation, and renewal were built. Understanding it is essential to understanding what was lost, what survived, and what was transformed.

Chapter Three
Contact with Europeans: First Meetings, Disease, and Survival

When strangers arrived by the hundreds of thousands, the world of Native peoples changed in ways that, at the time, no one could have fully predicted. Trade, curiosity, and cautious friendship marked many first encounters. In short order those meetings opened a door to exchange and innovation. They also opened a door to devastation: disease, dispossession, and conflict that reshaped entire regions. This chapter follows the arc of first contact, shows how communities responded, and highlights the strategies that helped some survive and adapt.

The First Meetings

First contact was rarely a single, dramatic moment. It happened differently in each region, at different times, and with different consequences. On the Atlantic coast, Columbus's arrival in 1492 set off a cascade of interactions between island peoples and European sailors. Along the eastern seaboard, fishermen and traders met Algonquian-speaking peoples, exchanging tools, cloth, and stories. Farther north, Norse explorers had brief contact with groups around Newfoundland centuries earlier. Along the Pacific and Gulf coasts, other encounters would follow with Spanish, French, Dutch, Portuguese, and later British explorers.

The early pattern was often cautious curiosity.
Native communities tested whether newcomers were
a threat, a source of goods, or both. Gifts were
exchanged. Language barriers were bridged by
gestures, shared work, and intermediaries. In some
cases, temporary alliances formed. In others,
misunderstandings and competing interests led to
tension. The range of outcomes was wide, but
certain features began to appear wherever
Europeans settled.

Trade and Technology: New Goods, New Dependencies

One of the most immediate effects of contact was
trade. European metal goods—for example, iron
knives, axes, kettles, and nails—arrived and quickly
became prized. Flint and bone tools were not
suddenly worthless, but metal tools made some
tasks easier. Cloth and woven goods transformed
clothing choices. Glass beads and mirrors became
items of exchange and cultural meaning. In regions
connected to coastal trade routes, Indigenous
peoples learned to navigate new markets, often
using long-standing trade networks to move
European goods inland.

At the same time, trade changed local economies
and dependencies. The fur trade in the Northeast
and Great Lakes regions illustrates this clearly.
European demand for beaver pelts turned hunting
into commerce on a scale never seen before. Some
tribes gained great wealth and bargaining power.

Others saw resources depleted and social patterns shift. The fur trade introduced guns and alcohol into societies that had not known them before. These changes had complex effects: firearms changed hunting and warfare, while alcohol created social problems for communities unprepared for its presence.

Another profound innovation was the horse. After Spanish horses escaped in the Southwest and on the Plains, tribes like the Comanche adopted them rapidly. The horse transformed mobility, hunting, and warfare. Tribes that integrated the horse into their culture adapted quickly and often gained an advantage in competition for land and resources. Technology was a two-edged sword: it offered new power and new vulnerabilities.

The Invisible Enemy: Disease and Demographic Collapse

Trade brought goods, but it also brought invisible carriers of disease. Smallpox, measles, influenza, and other Eurasian illnesses swept across the hemisphere with devastating speed. Native peoples had no immunity to these pathogens because they had not lived alongside them for centuries, as Europeans had. The result was catastrophic. In some regions mortality rates ranged from 50 to 90 percent. Whole villages emptied. Elders and knowledge keepers died. Agricultural knowledge, songs, and the memory of specific local places sometimes vanished with them.

The demographic collapse reshaped power and landscape. Empty fields reverted to forest. Long-distance trade networks fractured. Tribes weakened by disease were more vulnerable to coercion, pressure, and invasion. Some communities responded by consolidating survivors into larger settlements. Others completely relocated. The scale of loss is hard to overstate: the social fabric itself was under attack, and survival meant more than outrunning an invading army. It meant reweaving community life.

Diplomacy, Alliances, and the Price of Peace

As European colonies grew, Indigenous leaders faced new political choices. Some sought alliances with European powers to protect themselves against rival tribes. The Iroquois Confederacy, for example, carved out a role as middlemen in trade and diplomacy. They negotiated with both the French and the British, using their strategic position to gain goods and political space. Other tribes allied with Europeans against traditional enemies, accepting guns and trade concessions in return.

Alliances helped some tribes survive in the short term, but they often came with heavy costs. European promises were unreliable. Treaties were written in foreign languages and interpreted through different legal systems. What one side saw as a temporary agreement could be read by the other as permanent land transfer. Diplomacy *required nimble negotiation and sometimes painful tradeoffs: survival strategies that forced elders to choose between two bad options.*

Culture in Motion: Adaptation and Resistance

Contact did not mean immediate surrender of culture. Native societies adapted in creative ways. Some adopted new crops brought from Europe and Africa, such as wheat or certain fruits, blending them with traditional plants. Others integrated European tools and weapons into their cultural practices, using them to defend village life or to refine crafts.

At the same time, resistance took many forms. Some groups fought militarily against encroachment. Others used legal avenues, petitioning colonial courts or later national governments to assert rights and protect land. Still others preserved culture quietly, teaching language and ceremonies in private, or embedding traditional practices in Christian worship. Survival often meant blending strategies: adapt in some ways, resist in others, and protect what mattered most.

One striking example is the role of women in cultural survival. In many tribes, women controlled seed saving and food production. During times of upheaval, they often kept knowledge alive through ceremonies, recipes, and child-rearing practices.

Their work sustained communities both physically and spiritually.

Missionaries, Schools, and the Attack on Culture

Religion played a critical role when the newcomers began a push to convert Indigenous peoples. Missionaries offered new spiritual frameworks and often provided basic services like schooling and medicine. For some families, conversion meant material support and increased security. For others, it meant cultural loss.

A darker element emerged in the 19th and 20th centuries, when governments implemented assimilationist policies. Boarding schools forced children away from families, punished native languages, and taught that their culture was inferior. These programs aimed to erase Indigenous identity. The psychological and cultural damage was profound and multigenerational. Survivors often returned with fractured relationships to family and community, while the loss of language among children weakened cultural continuity.

Land, Law, and the Erosion of Territory

European concepts of land ownership clashed with Indigenous worldviews. Where Indigenous peoples saw land as communal and relational, European settlers saw it as a commodity to be owned, surveyed, and traded. This difference in perspective made negotiations difficult. Treaties often contained ambiguous language. Colonizers used maps, legal instruments, and force to claim territory.

Colonial and later national governments created laws that dispossessed tribes. Some tribes were pushed onto smaller reservations, others were moved far from ancestral homelands. These legal and military pressures rearranged demographics and broke traditional land-based practices. The loss of hunting ground and sacred places upended social and spiritual life.

Survival Strategies that Endured

Despite overwhelming odds, many communities found ways to endure. Some strategies proved especially important.

1. *Rebuilding through kinship ties. Displaced families often reformed networks with distant relatives. Kinship provided practical help and emotional stability.*
2. *Adopting selective technology. Guns, horses, and metal tools were used where they supported traditional goals: better hunting, defense, and craft production.*
3. *Legal and political savvy. Some tribes learned to use colonial and national legal systems to defend rights. Legal petitions, treaties, and negotiations became tools for survival.*

4. *Cultural quiet preservation. Language and ceremony sometimes survived underground. Elders passed stories and songs to families despite prohibition. Those private acts of resistance kept cultural memory alive.*
5. *Alliances with sympathetic outsiders. Some European settlers and later Americans supported Indigenous rights. Allies in missions, academia, or government sometimes helped preserve language, record oral histories, or push back against land grabs.*

Stories of Response

Stories help us understand what statistics cannot. Consider the family who buried their most sacred items rather than hand them to soldiers. Consider councils that debated whether to fight, flee, or negotiate. Consider the children who hid their native speech until adulthood, then taught it to their own children decades later. These small acts collectively preserved identity.

One often-told story is of a small coastal tribe that, after losing most of its elders to disease, used newly forged alliances to control access to a vital fishing spot. By negotiating with a colonial port town, they secured enough rights to continue their fisheries and feed remaining families. It was not a victory in the sense of restoring all that was lost, but it was a pragmatic step that preserved life and culture.

Practical Lessons for Readers

History offers concrete lessons for today. If you want to act respectfully and usefully when engaging with Indigenous histories and communities, consider these steps.

1. *Learn before you act. Read primary Indigenous voices. Contemporary Native authors give perspective that secondhand accounts do not.*
2. *Support Indigenous-led initiatives. Whether it is language revitalization, cultural centers, or legal defense funds, Indigenous organizations often know best how to use outside support.*
3. *Visit thoughtfully. If you visit a reservation or cultural site, follow local protocols. Buy from Native artists and ask how to engage in a culturally sensitive way.*
4. *Advocate for accurate teaching. In local schools and libraries, encourage curricula that present Indigenous history in context, with emphasis on Indigenous agency and voices.*
5. *Preserve stories. If you collect oral histories, do so with permission and with plans to return copies to communities.*

These are small but meaningful choices that shift public memory from exoticization toward respect.

Looking Ahead

Contact brought rapid, often violent change. It also opened pathways for adaptation that some communities used to survive. The story of those first centuries after contact is not simply one of loss. It is a complex mix of trade, disease, diplomacy, resistance, and resilience. Knowing this complexity is essential to understanding what followed.

The next chapter turns to the full weight of those consequences. It examines forced removals, wars over land, broken treaties, and the policies that aimed to erase Indigenous life. It is a chapter about the struggle for survival at scale, and about the strategies communities used to hold onto what mattered most. As you read that chapter, keep in mind the choices leaders and families faced in the decades after first contact. Their decisions shaped not just survival, but the path for generations to come.

Chapter Four
The Struggle for Survival: Wars, Removals, and Resilience

When contact first began, some encounters were tentative and even cooperative. Within a few generations, however, patterns of displacement, violence, and legal pressure took hold. This chapter traces how those pressures became a sustained struggle for survival. It looks at the wars fought, the treaties broken, the forced removals that emptied valleys and hollowed villages, and the policies that tried to erase language and culture. It also looks at how people persisted: the small acts of defiance and everyday practices that kept communities intact even in the darkest years.

When Peace Turned to Conflict

Conflict between Native communities and European settlers came in many shapes. Sometimes it was over immediate needs, like food, hunting ground, or water rights. Other times it was driven by expanding settlements and clashing worldviews about land. What might begin as a dispute over where a road would run could quickly escalate into violence because the balance of power had shifted. Colonists had growing military capacity, and governments were increasingly willing to use it.

Early resistance was often local and pragmatic. Tribes defended their villages, formed alliances, or withdrew to safer territory. Leaders had to weigh the cost of war against the needs of children and elders. War was not romantic. It was a brutal disruption of daily life, with long-term consequences for families and food supplies.

Forced Removals and Broken Promises

Perhaps the most devastating policy was removal. Throughout the eighteenth and nineteenth centuries, governments pushed tribes from ancestral lands to territories often far from home. These removals were never simply relocations. They were acts that severed spiritual ties to place, undermined traditional food systems, and shattered community networks.

One of the clearest examples is the mass displacement of southeastern tribes. Treaties that promised protection and land were reinterpreted, ignored, or enforced by force. Families were told to leave ancestral towns and walk hundreds of miles across unfamiliar terrain. Many did not survive the journey because of hunger, exposure, or disease. Graves along the way are stark proof of that suffering. Removal turned communities inward, forcing them to rebuild from the ground up in new, often hostile surroundings.

War and Massacre

When removals and broken treaties met resistance, the result was sometimes open warfare. Battles, raids, and massacres left scars that lasted generations. Military campaigns burned crops and villages. Men who could fight often did, not as lovers of war but as protectors of home and family. Other times, the balance of power was so unequal that massacres followed. Noncombatants—women, children, and elders—paid a dreadful price in those moments.

These events were not isolated to a single region or a single century. They repeated in different forms wherever settlers pushed for land and resources. The memory of slaughter and betrayal was kept alive in stories, songs, and family histories. Those memories shaped how communities responded in subsequent decades. They also shaped the way descendants remembered identity and justice.

Law as a Tool of Dispossession

Colonial and national laws increasingly supported the removal of Native people from land. Land surveys, property deeds, and court rulings created a legal language that often excluded Indigenous concepts of shared land. Treaties were written in terms that made sense to European officials, and when those treaties did not suit settler interests, they were ignored or reinterpreted.

Reservation systems grew out of these legal changes. In many places, reservations were intended as places where tribes would be contained, managed, and assimilated. Reservations could be remote, with poor soil and limited access to traditional resources. They also mixed together people from different nations who had not shared a homeland or history. The result was social strain and economic hardship.

At the same time, some leaders turned to legal advocacy. They petitioned courts, negotiated treaties, and used whatever legal means were available to protect remaining lands. Over time, law also became a battleground for recognition, sovereignty, and rights. The fight for justice shifted between the battlefield, the negotiation table, and the courthouse.

The Attack on Culture: Schools and Assimilation

Beyond land and life, colonizers launched a sustained campaign against culture. Assimilation policies aimed to remake Native identity. Boarding schools became a central instrument of that campaign. Children were removed from families and placed in institutions that told them their language, dress, and stories were wrong. They were punished for speaking native tongues. Their ceremonies were forbidden.

This was cultural violence. It sought to cut the roots of identity. The psychological harm was profound. Children returned with habits that estranged them from elders. Languages were lost. The transmission of songs, medicines, and stories slowed or stopped entirely. For many families, the cost was not only in a generation of disrupted knowledge but in the way that trauma passed from parent to child.

Still, community members resisted in ways big and small. Some parents hid language lessons at home. Elders taught children in secret. Some teachers in those schools quietly preserved words and stories. This quiet resistance kept the possibility of revival alive, even when institutions worked to suppress it.

Economic Displacement and Everyday Survival

Loss of homeland also meant loss of access to food and livelihoods. Hunting grounds were fenced, rivers were dammed, and access to traditional medicines declined. Economic marginalization became a long-term reality for many. Poverty, overcrowding, and limited access to healthcare and education followed.

Communities responded with practical strategies. Some turned to wage labor in nearby towns. Others adapted agricultural practices to new soils. Cooperative systems developed to share scarce resources. What could have been sheer devastation sometimes became the basis for creative survival strategies. People pooled labor for planting and harvesting. They revived crafts for sale to sustain families. In many places, the same ingenuity that had once supported life in place now supported life in motion.

Cultural Preservation and Adaptation

*Forced removal did not always mean cultural end.
Where possible, communities preserved rituals,
songs, and stories. In some cases, cultural practices
were adapted to new conditions. Ceremonies were
shortened or moved to different landscapes.
Traditional songs were recorded where elders
would sing them for later generations. Crafts were
turned into economic lifelines through trade with
settlers and later tourists.*

*Religious syncretism also occurred. Missionary
Christianity blended with traditional beliefs in some
places, producing new spiritual forms that allowed
people to maintain identity while navigating new
pressures. At the same time, the revival movements
of the late nineteenth and twentieth centuries
rekindled interest in traditional practices and
languages.*

Leadership and Resistance Movements

*Leadership during these hard years took many
forms. Some leaders sought accommodation,
believing it would save lives and secure a future.
Others insisted on armed resistance, preferring to
fight for homeland no matter the cost. Both choices
came at terrible price. Political leaders had to make
impossible decisions under the pressure of hunger,
disease, and military threat.*

Resistance movements also evolved. Where arms failed, legal and political strategies took their place. Tribal leaders and advocates worked to build alliances, appeal to national consciences, and lobby legislatures for rights and recognition. The work was slow and often frustrating, but it created the groundwork for later movements that fought for self-determination and legal redress.

Small Acts That Kept Culture Alive

Not all acts of survival involved treaties or battles. Many were small and private. Families preserved songs in lullabies. Crafts were hidden away in trunks. Language was spoken softly among relatives. These private acts were the seeds of later revival.

One common response was the stubborn refusal to abandon story. Oral histories were memorized and taught in secret. Names of sacred places were recited quietly. Even during periods when public ceremonies were forbidden, people found ways to mark seasons and births. When the moment came to reclaim those practices, these private reserves of knowledge became the core of cultural renewal.

Stories of Resilience

Stories reveal more than facts. Think of a family that, after a forced march, rebuilt a garden in a new landscape using knowledge of native seeds and soil. Or consider a community that collected elders' *stories and turned them into a book, handing it to a new generation. In each case, resilience looks less like a single heroic act and more like repeated, quiet choices to keep language, foodways, and ceremony alive.*

Another story is about people who used the legal system to reclaim land or rights. These victories were often partial, but they proved that the tools of the colonizers could sometimes be turned back against them. Activists used petitions, testimonies, and international attention to press for restitution. Those efforts carried risk, but they also created hope.

Practical Steps for Readers

If this chapter leaves you unsettled, that is the right reaction. History is messy and often painful. Here are some practical steps you can take to learn and to support living communities.

1. *Read Indigenous accounts. First-person narratives and writings by Native historians give voice to what official records often hide. Start with memoirs, oral history collections, and contemporary Indigenous scholars.*
2. *Support cultural preservation. Donate to or volunteer with language revitalization programs, cultural centers, and museums run by Indigenous organizations.*

3. *Learn local history. Many communities have local records, tribal museums, and elders willing to share stories. Respect protocols and ask how best to learn.*
4. *Advocate for accurate education. Encourage fair representation of Indigenous history in schools, libraries, and public spaces.*
5. *Practice mindful remembrance. When you visit historical sites, consider the human stories behind markers and plaques. Reflect on whose voices are present and whose are missing.*

Looking Ahead

This chapter has sketched a difficult arc: war, removal, cultural suppression, and the many forms of survival that emerged in response. The story does not end here. Next, we will explore how those threads of resistance, creativity, and quiet preservation wove into revival in the modern era. We will look at language reclamation, political resurgence, cultural renaissance, and the ways young people are reshaping identity today. The past is always with us, but it does not determine the future. The next chapter shows how communities have taken what was left and built new life from it.

Chapter Five
Legacy, Resilience, and Modern Identity

If the previous chapters traced arrival, daily life, contact, and the worst years of removal and suppression, this chapter looks at what came after: the hard, steady work of rebuilding. It is a chapter about survival that turned into renewal. It is also about identity, and how people who once risked losing everything found new ways to keep their cultures alive, claim rights, and shape the modern world on their own terms.

Carrying the Past into the Present

Survival after trauma is not a single moment. It is a thousand small decisions repeated across time. A family hides a prayer bundle in an attic. An elder whispers a song to a child. A group of friends meets quietly to practice a dance that was forbidden in public. Those private acts knit together what public policies tried to tear apart.

In the twentieth century, many Native people moved into towns and cities in search of work. That movement carried practices into new spaces. Urban Indians formed community centers where they taught language and crafts. Others organized politically to push back against policies that continued to undermine sovereignty. The story of revival is therefore also the story of adaptation. It is not about returning to a past world in all its detail. It is about selecting what to keep, reshaping what was lost, and creating something living and new.

Legal and Political Turnarounds

Law became both a tool of oppression and a tool of recovery. In the mid-twentieth century, Native leaders began using courts, federal legislation, and political organizing to press for rights. Some of the most consequential changes came from inside governments, when Indigenous advocates and allies won reforms that recognized tribal sovereignty in new ways.

One important shift came with laws that encouraged self-governance. These laws gave tribes more control over education, health services, and local resources. Where assimilation had once been the stated goal of policy, the new approach recognized the right of tribes to govern themselves and to run programs for their own communities. That was not a quick fix. It required institutions, training, and resources. It also required a new kind of political literacy among tribal leaders who now had to navigate complex funding systems and legal frameworks.

At the same time, landmark legal battles forced governments to confront past wrongs. Lawsuits and negotiations recovered some lands, clarified treaty obligations, and established precedents for compensation. Those victories were rarely complete, but they mattered. They returned a measure of dignity and practical relief to communities that had been pushed to the margins.

Cultural Revival and Language Reclamation

One of the most powerful signs of resilience is language revival. Language holds more than vocabulary. It carries worldviews, place names, songs, and ceremonial instructions. When a language dies, a unique way of seeing the world goes with it.

Throughout the late twentieth and early twenty-first centuries, many tribes launched immersion schools, community classes, and digital programs to teach children their ancestral tongues. Some efforts involved elders recording stories for younger speakers. Others created apps, online dictionaries, and translated materials for classrooms. The process of language revival also fostered pride. Young people who once learned only English began to take up their languages as a way of reconnecting to identity.

Cultural practices returned as well. Powwows, once driven underground or discouraged, became public celebrations. Regalia, dances, and songs that had been suppressed were reclaimed and shared with a wider audience. Museums that once displayed artifacts without context began collaborating with tribes to curate exhibits in ways that honored original meanings. That shift changed how the public saw Native cultures. Instead of frozen relics of the past, they appeared as living, evolving traditions.

Arts, Literature, and New Voices

Modern Native artists and writers brought another form of revival. Through novels, film, painting, and music, they told stories from inside communities rather than through outside imagination. Authors like Louise Erdrich and Joy Harjo, among many others, placed Native experience into mainstream culture. Their work offered nuance, complexity, and challenge to stereotyped images.

Contemporary visual artists used traditional motifs in new media. Filmmakers explored history and identity through both documentary and fiction. Musicians blended ceremonial rhythms with modern genres. This creative energy did more than entertain. It changed public conversation and created spaces where identity could be explored and celebrated.

Economic Self-Determination

Economic life also shifted. Tribal enterprises— ranging from small craft businesses to large enterprises in energy, hospitality, and technology— became engines for community support. Revenues from tribal businesses funded schools, healthcare, and cultural programs. Some tribes reinvested profits into language programs and land stewardship. Others created partnerships with universities and private companies to build capacity.

Economic sovereignty is complicated. Not every enterprise succeeds. Outside investment can bring tough choices about cultural integrity. Still, where tribes managed to balance business sense with community values, economic development empowered local control. It reduced dependence on external agencies and created more options for younger people who wanted to live on or near their homelands.

Environmental Leadership and Stewardship

One place where traditional knowledge and modern policy met successfully is environmental stewardship. Many tribes led movements to protect land and water. Their approaches often combined scientific methods with traditional ecological knowledge. That combination proved powerful in addressing issues like species protection, water quality, and forest management.

Indigenous leadership often framed stewardship around long-term responsibility rather than short-term profit. That perspective influenced wider conservation efforts and, in some cases, led to successful legal battles to protect sacred places from development. It also inspired partnerships between tribes and conservation organizations that respect both scientific and cultural values.

Youth, Identity, and the Future

Young Native people are the bridge between past and future. They bring new perspectives and tools— social media, graphic design, entrepreneurship— while often seeking deeper cultural roots. Many young people are relearning language and ceremony, sometimes after long family gaps. They are also reshaping identity in creative ways, blending traditional practices with contemporary life.

This generational renewal matters not only for culture but for politics. Young organizers lead movements on issues such as environmental protection, education reform, and cultural recognition. They bring energy, tech skills, and new networks to old problems. Their leadership suggests

*that the story of survival is not ending. It is
unfolding.*

Ongoing Challenges

*Renewal does not mean the problems are solved.
Many communities still face poverty, inadequate
health care, and underfunded schools. Issues like
infrastructure, housing, and mental health remain
pressing. The legacy of past policies—
intergenerational trauma, disrupted families, and
lost languages—cannot be erased quickly.*

*Political challenges persist. Disputes over land,
water rights, and jurisdiction remain. Some treaty
obligations have still not been fully honored. Tribal
governments often work within constrained legal
frameworks that limit their authority or funding.
Those constraints create daily struggles that coexist
with cultural revival.*

*The modern world also brings new pressures.
Climate change threatens traditional food sources
and sacred sites. Economic shifts can undermine
local businesses. Social media can both connect
communities and amplify conflict. The long view,
however, suggests that these challenges are being
met with the same combination of creativity and
stubbornness that has carried Indigenous peoples
through earlier crises.*

Practical Ways Readers Can Support
Renewal

If you want to support Indigenous resilience in concrete ways, here are practical actions that respect agency and culture.

1. *Listen to Indigenous voices. Read contemporary Native writers and follow Native-led media. Prioritize first-person accounts over outsider interpretations.*
2. *Support Indigenous organizations. Donate to language programs, cultural centers, or legal defense funds run by tribes. These organizations often know best how to use resources.*
3. *Buy directly from Native artists and makers. Purchasing crafts and books from creators provides income and affirms cultural value.*
4. *Advocate for policy change. Encourage local and national leaders to honor treaty obligations, support tribal sovereignty, and fund programs that tribes request.*
5. *Engage ethically with cultural sites. When visiting sacred places or museums, follow tribal protocols and ask how to show respect.*

These steps move support beyond goodwill. They make it practical and accountable.

Stories That Point the Way

Stories of revival are both small and grand. One community rebuilt a language program by inviting elders into schools and paying them for their time.

Another used revenue from a tribal business to fund a land buyback program, restoring parcels that had been sold off generations earlier. A group of artists formed a cooperative that supported young makers and turned traditional designs into sustainable income. Each story shows how practical choices can lead to meaningful recovery.

Looking Ahead

The legacy of Native peoples is not fixed. It changes with each generation that chooses what to remember and what to reinvent. In that sense, revival is not a return. It is a creative act. It takes courage to hold both grief and pride. It takes skill to make a living while honoring cultural forms. It takes imagination to turn past lessons into future solutions.

The next chapter will go deeper into language, law, and land. It will examine concrete programs that are bringing languages back, legal cases that are reshaping rights, and community projects that protect sacred places. If this chapter showed how renewal looks in broad strokes, the next one will offer the tools and tactics that make renewal possible.

Visual elements to include with this chapter

1. *A timeline of key legal and policy milestones relevant to self-determination and cultural revival.*
2. *Photographs of contemporary cultural gatherings, such as powwows or language immersion classrooms, credited to creators or tribal archives.*
3. *A sidebox case study: a short profile of a successful tribal enterprise or language program, with figures and outcomes.*
4. *An art spread showing modern Native artists who blend traditional motifs with new media.*

Would you like me to draft Chapter Six next, focusing on language revival, legal cases, and land restoration projects with concrete examples and resources?

Chapter Six
Language, Land, and Law: Reclaiming What Was Lost

If revival has a practical face, you see it in three places: the words people hear at home, the parcel of land a community protects, and the courtrooms where rights are defended. This chapter follows those three threads—language revival, land restoration, and legal victories—and shows how each thread strengthens the others. These are not abstract victories. They are the daily work of elders teaching children, councils buying back small parcels of ancestral ground, and lawyers and activists forcing governments to honor promises. Together they form the repair work of a people rebuilding what was taken.

The Sound of Return: Language Revival

Language carries more than grammar. It carries a people's history, place names, songs, and ceremonies. When a language dies, a way of seeing the world dies with it. That is why language revival has been one of the most emotional and effective fronts of cultural renewal.

Some of the most inspiring success stories are grassroots. The Wôpanâak (Wampanoag) Language Reclamation Project began with elders, linguists, and community members piecing together a language that had not been spoken fluently for generations. Through careful study of colonists' records, songs, and old documents, the project created curricula and immersion classes that brought children into the language again. That work shows that reclamation is possible even after decades of suppression. (JMU Scholarly Commons)

Models for revival vary. The Master-Apprentice approach pairs fluent elders with motivated learners in daily, immersive practice. It is simple, low cost, and rooted in shared activity—cooking, crafting, farming—so language learning becomes part of life rather than a classroom exercise. Programs modeled on that approach have spread across North America because they fit small communities and build intergenerational bonds. (Brill, Wikipedia)

Technology and modern platforms have also joined the effort. Universities now offer certificate programs for language teachers, and apps and online courses widen access for diaspora communities who cannot live near elders. Duolingo and other platforms, for example, have launched courses in Indigenous languages such as Navajo, creating low-barrier entry points for curious learners and younger generations who live far from home. (navajo.unm.edu, Duolingo)

Revival work is rarely glamorous. It involves transcribing elders' speech, inventing new words for modern objects, creating children's books, and securing funds for immersion schools. Yet these small, steady actions produce generational change.

When a child answers a question in their ancestral tongue, the air in the room changes. Identity shifts from something remembered to something spoken.

Land Back: Buybacks, Monuments, and Return

Language is tied to place. Place names, stories about springs and rocks, and seasonal harvest calendars are encoded in the landscape. Recovering control over land therefore became a clear priority for many tribes.

One federal program tied directly to this work is the Land Buy-Back Program for Tribal Nations. Implemented under the Cobell settlement, the program buys fractional interests in trust land from willing sellers, consolidates holdings, and restores whole parcels to tribal trust ownership. It is practical work—small purchases that add up to restored control over traditional land. For many communities, that consolidation matter means regaining the ability to manage sacred sites, to reestablish seasonal harvesting, and to make land-based cultural practices possible again. (U.S. Department of the Interior)

Other victories come through political action. Restoring national monument status to places like Bears Ears in Utah recognized both the ecological and cultural importance of the land and formalized protections after years of pressure from tribes and allies. These victories are symbolic and practical:

they protect archaeological sites, provide a legal basis for tribal consultation, and re-center Indigenous stewardship in federal decision making. (Federal Register)

Beyond federal action, tribal land buybacks, purchases from willing sellers, and cooperative management agreements with federal agencies have become tangible ways for communities to reclaim place. Each acre returned is another story that can be told in the language of the people who lived there before.

Courts and Treaties: Law as a Tool for Redress

If language and land are about culture and place, law is often the instrument through which rights are enforced. Over the past decades, a string of legal decisions has reshaped how government and courts recognize tribal authority.

One landmark ruling came from the U.S. Supreme Court in McGirt v. Oklahoma, which confirmed that large parts of eastern Oklahoma remain Indian country because Congress had not disestablished the reservation. The decision had immediate and practical consequences for jurisdiction, criminal prosecution, and the affirmation of treaty promises. It also served as a clarion call: treaties and statutes still matter, and where the law recognizes reservation status, tribal sovereignty follows. (The Guardian, Oklahoma Bar)

Another significant legal issue involved the Indian Child Welfare Act (ICWA), which sets federal standards for child welfare cases involving Native children. In challenges that reached the Supreme Court as Haaland v. Brackeen, the law's central protections were affirmed. That ruling reinforced the idea that protecting Native families and keeping children connected to culture are federal priorities—not optional policies. For communities recovering from generations of forced removal and boarding-school separation, legal wins like this preserve the social fabric critical to cultural continuity. (Native American Rights Fund, Oklahoma Bar)

Law is not always a straight path to justice, but it is a vehicle. Courts, statutes, and negotiated settlements have returned land, affirmed jurisdiction, and sometimes compelled governments to act. At their best, legal tools legitimize the claims communities have made for generations.

How These Threads Strengthen Each Other

The work of language revival, land recovery, and legal affirmation is mutually reinforcing. A consolidated parcel of land provides a place where summer immersion classes can happen. Legal recognition of reservation status gives tribes practical authority to manage land and schools. Language programs deepen the community's claim to place—children who learn local place names become natural advocates for protecting them.

Consider a small reservation that secures a piece of ancestral forest through a buyback. The council uses that land for language immersion camps in summer, paying elders as instructors. That practice strengthens cultural life, provides work, and builds political capital to press for further legal protections. The gains multiply.

Concrete Examples and Resources

Here are concrete models and resources that communities and allies have used:

• Master-Apprentice programs and immersion schools for language learning. These pair elders with committed learners and build daily practice into everyday tasks. (Brill, Wikipedia)

• Federal programs such as the Land Buy-Back Program for Tribal Nations, which purchases fractional interests and restores them to tribal trust ownership. (U.S. Department of the Interior)

• Monument restoration and cooperative management agreements like those around Bears Ears National Monument, where federal recognition created a framework for tribal consultation and protection. (Federal Register)

• University partnerships and certificate programs that train community members to teach language in schools and community programs. (*navajo.unm.edu*)

• Modern digital tools. Apps, online dictionaries, and language courses broaden reach—especially for urban and diaspora members seeking to reconnect. (*Duolingo*)

Practical Steps for Readers Who Want to Help

If you want to support this work in ways that matter, consider actions that are practical and accountable.

1. Support community-led projects. Donate to tribal language programs, cultural centers, and legal defense funds that are run by or in partnership with tribes.
2. Buy directly from Native makers and artists. Economic support sustains language teachers and cultural programs.
3. Read and amplify Indigenous voices. Learn from survivors, scholars, and artists who speak for their communities.
4. Show up respectfully. If you visit cultural sites, follow tribal protocols. If you record elders' stories, ask permission, and ensure the community receives copies.
5. Advocate for policy. Encourage local and national leaders to fund language programs,

*honor treaty obligations, and support land
buyback initiatives.*

*These steps move support from sympathy to
partnership.*

Stories That Point the Way

*A community that used land-buyback funds to buy a
small island in a river and turned it into a seasonal
camp produced one of the clearest success stories.
Elders led youth in canoe-making and language
classes, and once-a-year ceremonies reestablished
the island's role in the community calendar. Stories
like that are common enough now to suggest a
pattern: when land, language, and law come
together, cultural renewal becomes practical.*

Looking Ahead

*The work of reclamation is unfinished. There are
more languages to save, more parcels of land to
recover, and more legal promises to enforce. But
the strategies are clear: protect land, teach
language, and use law where it can help. The next
chapter will explore how cultural revival takes
public form—through arts, literature, and media—
and how new Native voices are reshaping national
narratives. If this chapter mapped the infrastructure
of resurgence, the next will show its visible, creative
face.*

Visual suggestions for this chapter

- *A case-study box showing before and after maps of a buyback parcel.*
- *Photos of a Master-Apprentice session or a language immersion classroom.*
- *A timeline of major legal milestones (McGirt, ICWA rulings, Cobell settlement, Bears Ears restoration).*
- *Resource sidebar with links to language programs, federal buyback information, and recommended Indigenous authors and organizations.*

Chapter Seven — New Voices: Art, Literature, and the Public Return of Indigenous Story

Art and story have always been central to Native life. Pottery, beadwork, song, dance, and carved totems carried history and meaning long before there were galleries, bookstores, or streaming festivals. In the last decades, however, those traditions moved into new public spaces. Native artists and writers took up contemporary forms to tell old stories and new ones. Museums began to display contemporary Native work as living practice, not just ethnographic relics. Poets and novelists from Indigenous communities reached national audiences, and powwows and festivals turned into powerful stages for identity and debate. This chapter looks at how that return to public life happened, why it matters, and how readers can engage respectfully and usefully.

When Tradition Meets Gallery Space

For a long time, mainstream art institutions treated Native creations as artifacts rather than contemporary art. That is changing. Major museums now mount shows that place Indigenous artists at the center of the conversation about modern art, not at the margins. Exhibitions have highlighted the work of painters, sculptors, photographers, and mixed media artists who use cultural motifs to ask urgent questions about history, identity, and power. These shows have helped shift public perception, making visible the fact that Native art evolves and responds to current events just like any other artistic practice. (National Museum of the American Indian, Smithsonian Institution)

Contemporary Native artists often work in multiple registers. A painter might reference traditional symbols while using modern color fields. A beadworker might translate ancestral patterns into installations that comment on consumer culture. That hybrid practice forces viewers to confront two assumptions at once: that Indigenous cultures are living and that contemporary art need not cut itself off from political and spiritual concerns.

One clear sign of this shift is the growth of museums and programs dedicated to contemporary Indigenous work. Institutions that once displayed only historical objects now curate living artists in rotating exhibitions and purchase contemporary pieces for permanent collections. The presence of work by Native artists in mainstream museums opens doors. It creates audiences that might never otherwise encounter these stories. It also gives artists platforms from which to speak directly to larger publics. (Institute of American Indian Arts (IAIA), National Museum of the American Indian)

Storytellers: Novelists, Poets, and the Native Renaissance

If visual art opened one door, literature threw the next one wide. Starting in the late twentieth century, a wave of Indigenous writers began publishing work that reached broad audiences. Poets and novelists wrote from inside their communities with urgency and nuance. Their books did not ask permission to exist in the mainstream; they simply told the truth of contemporary Native life, mixing mythic memory with modern experience.

Poets such as Joy Harjo brought Native perspectives into the national conversation. Her position as United States poet laureate signaled that Indigenous voices were not peripheral. Novelists like Louise Erdrich offered narratives that threaded family history with community politics, memory with legal struggle. Their work helped create what many scholars and readers call a Native renaissance in literature, a moment when Indigenous storytelling reclaimed space in the cultural imagination. (The Poetry Foundation, Reedsy)

What makes this literature powerful is its authority. These are not outsider interpretations. They are inside voices that narrate complexity. They speak about grief and humor, law and love, land and language. Readers who come to these books encounter layered lives, not tokens of exoticism. For the culture at large, the effect is clarifying. Indigenous writers are shaping national memory and teaching audiences to listen differently.

Performance and the Powwow Stage

Public performance is another place where Native identity asserts itself. Powwows, once a response to displacement and a means of cultural continuity, now carry a complicated but vibrant life. They are gatherings that blend ceremony, competition, commerce, and community. For many people powwows are both a celebration of survival and a forum for negotiating authenticity in a commercial world. (folklife.si.edu, AP News)

At a powwow you see regalia that reflects family history, songs carried across generations, and dances that mark lineage and status. You also see younger performers experimenting with style, with drumming patterns borrowed or blended, with designs that respond to the visual language of the present. Powwows are an arena where the living tensions of culture are played out publicly and where elders and youth meet on common ground.

These gatherings are political as well. They are opportunities to teach visitors about history and meaning, to sell crafts that sustain artists, and to push back against stereotypes. They can also raise hard questions about appropriation, commercialization, and who gets to claim cultural forms. That complexity makes powwows important places to learn, but it also means visitors should approach with humility and respect.

Film, Music, and Media: Reclaiming the Camera and Microphone

Another front of cultural return is audiovisual media. Filmmakers from Indigenous communities are making documentaries and fiction films that center Native perspectives. They control narrative and imagery in ways that documentary crews of the past rarely did. Film and video bring ceremony and story to screens, reaching audiences that might never visit a museum or attend a powwow.

Music offers a similar trajectory. Artists blend traditional rhythms and instruments with hip hop, folk, and electronic styles. The result is work that refuses to be boxed as folk or world music. It asserts modern identity while remaining accountable to tradition. These artists often use their platforms to educate listeners about treaties, land issues, and the ongoing effects of settler policies.

Journalism and podcasting have also become important. Native-led media outlets and podcasts tell community news, share interviews with elders, and document revival projects. These platforms create archives of voices that can be used by educators, activists, and future storytellers.

Where Art Meets Activism

A striking feature of contemporary Indigenous art is its fusion of aesthetics and activism. Artists do not shy away from politics. Visual campaigns, installations, films, and performances have drawn attention to environmental fights, sovereignty *disputes, and human rights issues. Art gives form and feeling to legal and political struggles. It makes abstract grievances tangible.*

A recent example is work that responded to pipeline protests, where artists created banners, installations, and performances that made visible the spiritual stakes of water and land protection. The public face of those campaigns was often media images and striking artworks that helped build broader coalitions. Art humanized distant policy debates and mobilized sympathetic audiences.

That activist dimension is not new but it is more visible now. Museums and festivals have shown protest art. Writers have published essays and novels that carry urgent legal and moral questions. The creative sphere became a strategic front in larger movements.

Young Creators and the Future of Tradition

Young Native creators are central to this cultural turn. They bring fluency in both ancestral practice and contemporary tools. They know how to code, how to use social platforms, how to design a gallery website, and how to translate a song into a viral clip. That technological fluency gives revival projects reach and adaptability.

At the same time, younger artists often seek direct mentorship from elders, asking permission to use certain stories or regalia. That intergenerational work keeps revival grounded. It prevents cultural extraction while enabling innovation.

Practical Steps for Readers Who Want to Engage

If this chapter leaves you inspired, here are practical ways to support these creative movements without taking over them.

1. *Buy directly from Native creators. Look for artist cooperatives, tribal galleries, and verified online shops. Buying work provides direct economic support and recognizes artistic labor.*
2. *Read Indigenous authors and cite them in your teaching and conversations. Give space to first-person voices when recommending books.*
3. *Attend powwows and festivals respectfully. Learn the rules ahead of time, ask permission before photographing individuals, and support vendors.*
4. *Follow Native-led media and arts organizations on social media. Share their work rather than repackaging it.*
5. *Support Indigenous radio, museum programs, and film festivals with donations or volunteer time.*
6. *Advocate for representation in local institutions. Encourage libraries to stock*

*Indigenous literature and push galleries to
include Native artists.*

*These are actions that shift attention and resources
toward Indigenous agency rather than outside
interpretation.*

Stories That Teach

*Consider the artist who took family beadwork
patterns and used them in a large installation that
asked viewers to confront the history of boarding
schools. The work traveled to several museums and,
at each stop, the artist led community workshops
about the history behind the patterns. That
combination of art, education, and community work
turned aesthetic attention into sustained
understanding.*

*Or think of the poet who recorded elders' stories
and then used those recordings as the basis for a
spoken-word album. The album toured schools and
inspired language classes, connecting
contemporary audiences to ancestral cadences.*

*These stories show how art can be a bridge:
between elders and youth, between local community
and global audience, and between memory and
policy.*

Visual Elements and Practical Resources

For this chapter consider including:

- *Photo spreads of contemporary exhibitions and artist profiles, with permissions noted.*
- *A sidebar list of recommended Native authors, filmmakers, and musicians to start with.*
- *A short case study box on a recent powwow or festival and how it balanced tradition and commercialization, with links to responsible visitor guides.*
- *QR codes linking to artist interviews, music tracks, or short documentary clips.*

Looking Ahead

Art and story helped Indigenous peoples survive colonization and now help them shape their future. The next chapter will look at cultural infrastructure in more detail: schools, museums, legal organizations, and economic models that support long-term revival. If this chapter showed the public face of revival, the next will examine its foundations and how communities build institutions that sustain culture across generations.

Chapter Eight
Honor, Hope, and What Comes Next: Modern Identity and the Road Forward

If earlier chapters traced arrival, survival, loss, and revival, this chapter looks ahead. It asks how identity is being remade now, what resilience looks like in everyday life, and how communities and allies can build a future that honors the past. This is a chapter about choices: the choices young people make, the choices communities make about what to revive and what to change, and the choices readers can make if they want to stand in solidarity.

Identity in Motion

Identity is not a dusty artifact. It is a living thing that changes with each generation. Today you find people who carry their cultures into urban apartments, college classrooms, corporate boardrooms, and art studios. You meet elders teaching language in community centers and teenagers remixing drum songs for digital audiences. That mixture can feel paradoxical. A language immersion classroom may sit next to a social feed that strips tradition down to a single image. Both are part of the same story.

For many Indigenous people identity now means holding two things at once. It means honoring sacred relationships with land, ceremony, and kin. It also means working in professions that did not exist for previous generations. People are lawyers, scientists, teachers, entrepreneurs, and artists who bring ancestral knowledge into those roles. Their identity is not diluted by modern life. It is deepened by the way they insist on practice, memory, and voice in every space they enter.

The New Commons: Culture as Collective Strength

One of the most powerful shifts of the past decades is the emphasis on what I will call the new commons. Communities intentionally rebuild shared resources and institutions that serve multiple purposes at once. A language immersion school is not only a place for grammar lessons. It is a place where elders are paid for their knowledge, where children learn local place names, and where community members gather for seasonal events. A tribal-run business is not only a revenue stream. It is a training ground, a funding source for cultural programs, and a platform for political leverage.

This commons approach reframes resilience from private survival to collective flourishing. It recognizes that culture, law, and land support one another. Investing in language programs strengthens legal claims to place. Purchasing a parcel of ancestral land makes it possible to restore a fishing site and to teach youth how the river once ran. That kind of integrated strategy is practical and durable.

Young People as Cultural Stewards

Young people are the hinge of continuity. They carry technology fluency and new aesthetics, but they also seek meaning in the old ways. Many of them are intentional about learning language, ceremony, and craft. They are as likely to be found debugging code as they are discussing ancestral place names at a community dinner.

Youth leadership looks like this. A group of students starts a small language club that grows into an after-school program. A collective of young artists organizes a show where beadwork and digital projection meet. A youth council creates a campaign to protect a watershed, using social media to mobilize allies. These efforts matter because they form new pathways for culture to remain vital in a changing world.

Adults play a crucial role, too. Elders who mentor young people, community leaders who prioritize education and jobs, and parents who insist on teaching songs are the glue that holds these efforts together. Where mentorship is steady and intergenerational bonds are strong, cultural learning happens naturally.

Sovereignty, Governance, and Practical Power

Identity alone cannot secure the things communities need. Political power matters. Sovereignty is not an abstract claim. It is the ability to set local priorities for health, education, and land management. It is a legal and practical tool for communities to protect their way of life.

In recent years, many tribes have built the capacity to manage schools, police services, health clinics, and economic enterprises. Those institutions help communities make long-term plans rather than react to a crisis. They also create jobs that keep people close to home. When a tribe runs its schools, language and culture can be woven into curricula. When it runs health services, culturally appropriate care can reach people who otherwise go without.

The work of governance requires training, transparency, and a commitment to democratic practice. It also requires partnerships that respect tribal sovereignty rather than simply extract from it. Good governance makes cultural revival more than symbolic. It turns revival into a lived, manageable reality.

Economic Choices That Respect Culture

Economic development is essential for sustainable revival, but it can create tension. A common trap is to prioritize short-term revenue over cultural integrity. The most durable projects balance earning with stewardship. They ask hard questions before opening a business or signing a partnership. Who benefits? Does the project create lasting local capacity? Does it protect sacred places? Does it respect traditional values about resource use?

Examples of ethical enterprise include craft cooperatives that pay fair wages to artisans, renewable energy projects planned with tribal consent, and tourism that is small scale, community-run, and educational. The guiding principle is local control. When decisions are made by the people most affected, they are more likely to support culture and long-term resilience.

Environmental Stewardship and Climate Resilience

For many Indigenous communities, environmental stewardship is both tradition and strategy. Traditional ecological knowledge—about seasonal cycles, fire regimes, and sustainable harvest—has real practical value in a changing climate. Communities are leading on land management projects that combine science with local practices. They reintroduce controlled burns to reduce fire risk, restore wetlands that buffer floods, and lobby to protect watersheds that sustain fish runs.

Those efforts are also political. They strengthen arguments for land protection and they build alliances with conservation groups. They demonstrate that stewardship rooted in cultural practice is effective conservation. In many cases, Indigenous-led stewardship is the best local strategy for both environmental and cultural survival.

Healing Work: Addressing Intergenerational Trauma

Regeneration is not only cultural and legal. It is psychological. The harms of forced removal, boarding schools, and cultural suppression run deep through families. Addressing that is part of rebuilding.

Healing programs often combine traditional practices with modern therapy. Sweat lodges, talking circles, story work, and ceremony are used alongside counseling and substance abuse treatment. Community-led health programs that respect cultural protocols see better results than outside interventions that fail to understand local context.

Healing also includes truth telling. Public acknowledgement of past wrongs, memorials, and led community dialogues help restore dignity. They are not a fix, but they are a part of communal repair.

The Role of Allies: How Non-Indigenous Readers Can Help

If you are not Indigenous and you want to help, there are meaningful steps to take that avoid harm.

1. *Center Indigenous voices. Listen first. Read books by Indigenous authors and prioritize*

those voices in conversation and scholarship.

2. *Support tribal-led initiatives. Donate to projects run by tribes rather than external organizations unless those organizations are explicitly invited partners.*

3. *Buy directly from Native creators. This supports artists materially and culturally.*

4. *Advocate for policy and funding that tribes request. Lobbying for language program funding, fair treaty enforcement, and infrastructure support is useful when guided by tribal priorities.*

5. *Respect protocols. Ask permission before photographing ceremonies, before using cultural designs in commercial products, and before claiming knowledge. When in doubt, wait and learn.*

6. *Challenge stereotypes in your networks. When you hear a caricature or a simplified story about Indigenous peoples, push back with nuance.*

These actions build respectful relationships rather than transactional ones.

Practical Steps Readers Can Do Right Now

Here are five concrete things you can do this week.

1. *Read a book by a contemporary Indigenous author and share it with a friend. Let the author lead the conversation.*

2. *Find a local Indigenous cultural center or museum and ask how to volunteer in ways that they find helpful.*
3. *Buy a craft or piece of art directly from a Native maker. If you cannot find one locally, support verified online cooperatives.*
4. *Attend a public event, such as a lecture, exhibit, or powwow, and prepare by learning visitor etiquette first.*
5. *Contact your school board or library and ask that Indigenous history be taught with community-sourced materials.*

Small actions add up. They shift public memory from caricature to respect.

Stories That Point to a Better Future

Real progress often looks modest at first. A single classroom that begins an after-school language club may grow into a village-wide immersion program ten years later. A small land buyback can create a protected spring that brings back seasonal ceremonies to a community. A single artist with a popular film can change how an entire region thinks about history.

These changes are rarely headline-making in their early days, but they build durable power. They are cumulative. They are the work of many hands over years.

Toward a Living Conclusion

This book has traced a long arc. It began with migration and survival, moved through contact and loss, and followed revival as it took root in law, land, language, and culture. Chapter Eight brings those threads together. Identity is not a shrine to be preserved untouched. It is practice that must be carried forward, taught, argued for, and renewed.

The road ahead will not be easy. There will be setbacks. There will be debates about how to balance new opportunities with cultural responsibility. There will be laws to fight and funding to secure. There will also be countless quiet victories: a child singing in a language that had been silenced, a reclaimed patch of riverbank where fish return, or a new museum exhibition curated by the people whose ancestors made the objects.

If you take one thing from this chapter, let it be this. Respect is action. Pride is practice. Hope is not passive. It asks us to do something every day, however small, to keep culture alive and to honor commitments made to the people who have stewarded this land for millennia.

Visual suggestions for this chapter

- *Photo spread of youth language classes, with short captions describing activities.*

- *Infographic that links language programs, land buybacks, and legal victories as a mutually reinforcing cycle.*
- *Profile box with a short story of a community project that combined an economic enterprise with cultural programming.*
- *Resource list for readers: recommended Indigenous authors, community organizations, and guidance on respectful participation.*

Printable Two-Page Handout

Use: giveaway at talks, downloadable PDF for readers and teachers. Suggested print: A5 or A4, 11–12 pt serif for body, 14–16 pt for headings, 0.75 inch margins.

Carrying the Story Forward — Practical Resources and Actions

Short intro
This handout collects practical reading, organizations, classroom activities, and simple steps readers can take to support Indigenous cultural revival. Start small. Act respectfully. Prioritize Indigenous-led projects.

Annotated Reading List (starter selection)

- ***Braiding Sweetgrass*** *— Robin Wall Kimmerer*
  Science and Indigenous wisdom on reciprocity and ecology. Great for lessons on environmental stewardship.
- ***An Indigenous Peoples' History of the United States*** *— Roxanne Dunbar-Ortiz*
  A broad, Indigenous-centered account useful for classroom context and teacher background.
- ***House Made of Dawn*** *— N. Scott Momaday*
  A lyrical novel exploring identity and renewal.

- ***Ceremony*** — *Leslie Marmon Silko*
  A novel linking healing to ceremony and place.
- ***The Round House*** — *Louise Erdrich*
  A contemporary novel that weaves law, family, and community trauma.
- ***Crazy Brave*** — *Joy Harjo*
  A poet's memoir that connects personal history with public voice.
- ***There There*** — *Tommy Orange*
  An urban, modern perspective that challenges stereotypes.
- ***The Heartbeat of Wounded Knee*** — *David Treuer*
  A corrective to narratives of disappearance, blending history and reporting.

Recommended Organizations and Support Options

Support Indigenous-led groups whenever possible. Start by contacting local tribal offices or cultural centers.

- *Local tribal councils and cultural centers — ask how to help.*
- *Language and cultural institutes — donate or volunteer with immersion programs.*
- *Native-led legal and advocacy organizations — support treaty and family rights work.*
- *Arts cooperatives and artist collectives — buy direct to sustain makers.*

Tip: Ask how funds will be used and prefer tribal-run programs.

Short Lesson Plans (60–90 minutes)

1. Oral History Intro (60 min)
Objective: Treat oral history as a primary source. Play a short elder interview, map places mentioned, reflect in a short paragraph.

2. Language Mini-Immersion (90 min)
Objective: Experience language as living practice. Practice 5 greetings or place names, then write a two-line micro-story using one new word.

3. Art and Meaning (60–90 min)
Objective: Analyze one contemporary Indigenous artwork. Create a visual response and write a short artist statement.

Each plan: invite a local elder when possible, pay honorarium if invited.

Quick Actions for Readers and Teachers

1. *Read an Indigenous author this month and recommend their book to one person.*
2. *Buy a craft directly from a Native maker or verified cooperative.*
3. *Visit a tribal museum or cultural center. Ask about volunteer or donation needs.*

4. *Add Indigenous-authored texts to your syllabus or library list.*
5. *If attending a powwow or ceremony, learn visitor etiquette first and ask permission before photographing.*

Discussion Prompts for Class or Group

- *Which stereotype in the book surprised you? How did your view change?*
- *Which survival strategy did you find most compelling and why?*
- *How does language carry knowledge that English may not convey? Give an example.*
- *Which practical action will you commit to this month? How will you follow through?*

Ethics and Permissions

- *Always ask permission before recording stories or photographing ceremonies.*
- *Work through tribal offices or cultural centers for community projects.*
- *If you collect stories, return copies to the community and explain the intended use.*
- *Prefer partnership, not extraction.*

Further Activities and Projects

- *Build a local resources map of tribal centers and Indigenous bookstores.*

- *Launch a classroom oral history archive with community consent.*
- *Host a fundraiser to support a local language class and deliver funds through the tribe.*

One-Page Reading Guide for Book Groups

Use: handout for book club meetings, downloadable PNG or PDF.

The Red Indians — Quick Book Group Guide

Purpose: *prompt respectful discussion, encourage action, and provide one short activity.*

Opening (5 minutes)

One person reads aloud a short passage from the book that moved them. Keep it under 120 words.

Core Discussion Questions (45 minutes)

1. *What surprised you most in the book about daily life before contact?*
2. *How did the chapter on contact and disease change your understanding of early colonial impact?*
3. *Which revival example felt the most hopeful and why?*
4. *What concrete support could your group offer to a local Indigenous program?*

Split into pairs and pick one action from this list. Each pair drafts a two-step plan to carry it out within a month:

- *Read and share an Indigenous author with two friends.*
- *Invite a local Indigenous speaker to a school or community event.*
- *Buy and display one craft from a Native maker and share its story with your circle.*

Pairs report back: name the action and the first step.

Closing (5 minutes)

Each member names one concrete thing they will do in the next 30 days. Write it in the meeting note and follow up at the next session.

Quick Resource List (for the host)

- *Suggested opening readings: Joy Harjo, Louise Erdrich, Robin Wall Kimmerer.*
- *Where to buy art: tribal online co-ops, verified museum shops.*
- *Local contact step: call your regional tribal council office to ask about protocols for invitations.*

If you want, I can:

- *Export these into a printable two-page PDF and a separate one-page PDF reading guide, or*
- *Prepare them as ready-to-import text frames formatted for A5 in InDesign (or a simple Word/Pages file).*

Which export would you like: **PDFs** *or* **editable Word/Pages files***?*

Done — I created both files for you:

- *Download the two-page handout (PDF)*
- *Download the one-page reading guide (PDF)*

If you want the same content as editable Word or Pages files for layout tweaks, I can convert them next. Would you like that?

Printed in Dunstable, United Kingdom

75582613R00057

Robbie Cameron

A Story of Freedom

D. N. Curran

D. N. Curran

Robbie Cameron
Copyright © 2014 D. N. Curran
All rights reserved.

For information about the contents of this book, or
permission for reproducing portions of this book,
contact the author.

This is a work of fiction. Names, characters, places, and
incidents are the product of the author's imagination or
are used fictitiously. Any resemblance to actual persons,
living or dead, events, or locales is entirely coincidental.

Published in the United States of America

ISBN-13: 978-1500216368
ISBN-10: 1500216364